MIGRATION

CATH SENKER

W

FRANKLIN WATTS
LONDON • SYDNEY

First published in Great Britain in 2024 by Hodder & Stoughton
Copyright © Hodder & Stoughton, 2024

Produced for Franklin Watts by
White-Thomson Publishing Ltd
www.wtpub.co.uk

Editor: Cath Senker
Designer: Clare Nicholas
Series Designer: Dan Prescott

HB ISBN: 978 1 4451 8798 3
PB ISBN: 978 1 4451 8800 3
EB ISBN: 978 1 4451 8799 0

Franklin Watts
An imprint of
Hachette Children's Group
Part of Hodder & Stoughton
Carmelite House
50 Victoria Embankment
London EC4Y 0DZ

An Hachette UK Company
www.hachette.co.uk

www.hachettechildrens.co.uk
Printed in Dubai

Picture acknowledgements:
Alamy: Iain Masterton 5, dpa picture alliance 13, Penny Tweedie 19, Xinhua 29; Flickr: 20; Getty: Pierre Michel Jean/AFP 22, Joseph Eid/AFP 25, Minasse Wondimu Hailu/Anadolu Agency 26; Gerrie Purcell 17 inset; Cath Senker 17t; Shutterstock: A_McIntyre cover t, Manoej Paateel cover b, Mariangela Cruz 4, Edgloris Marys 6, Abd_Almohimen_Sayed 7, Nelson Antoine 8, Richard van der Spuy 9t, Cavan-Images 9b, Stcc 10, solmaz daryani 11, Dragana Gordic 12, Greg Patton 14, Ververidis Vasilis 15, Parikh Mahendra N 16, Luis Acosta 18, littlenySTOCK 21, corners74 23, Viktoria Bykanova 24, Jahangir Alam Onuchcha 27, Ibrahem Anas 28.

Author acknowledgements:
The author would like to acknowledge these major sources: IOM World Migration Report 2022; IOM World Migration Report 2020, chapter 5; Migrants, Refugees and Societies, World Bank 2023.

All design elements from Shutterstock.

CONTENTS

WHAT IS MIGRATION?

Throughout history, people have travelled to find food or water, or to escape natural disaster or conflict. Most moved within their own country. Some travelled to explore, trade or conquer other lands. From around 1500 CE Europeans voyaged afar to colonise vast areas of the Americas, Australia, Asia and Africa. Between 1850 and 1925, 50 to 60 million Europeans left their homelands for Australia, Canada, New Zealand, the USA and Argentina. International migration has continued ever since.

Migration today

Today, as in the past, most people move to another part of their country. If they can't find jobs in the countryside, they go to the city to find work. A minority depart for other countries. They may migrate for a short time, perhaps travelling to pick fruit at harvest time. Many Pakistanis, Indians and Bangladeshis work for a few years in the high-income Gulf States. Others move long-term: the wealthy USA is the top destination country for international migrants.

In the 19th century, German migrants settled in Hahndorf, a small town in South Australia. Village shops sell German cuckoo clocks and toys.

South Asian migrant building workers in Dubai, United Arab Emirates, get on the bus to go to their living quarters after work.

Forced migration

Some people are forced to migrate. From 1500 to 1870, Europeans enslaved around 12 million Africans and shipped them to the Caribbean and the Americas to work. Other people have escaped as refugees. When India was divided into Hindu-majority India and Muslim-majority Pakistan in 1947, around 15 million people fled from one to another. Between half and two million died in the resulting violence. In recent years, millions have escaped crises in Afghanistan, Syria, Venezuela, Ukraine, South Sudan, the Central African Republic and other lands.

This book looks at why people migrate, where they go, and what happens to them. We examine the positive and negative impacts on the countries that host them and those they leave behind.

IT'S A FACT

The number of international migrants has increased greatly over the last 50 years, but the proportion hasn't. In 2023, just 2.3 per cent of the global population lived in a different country to the one where they were born.

WHY DO PEOPLE MIGRATE?

People move because of push or pull factors, or a mixture of both. Pull factors are the good aspects of another country or area that encourage people to go there. Push factors are the problems that drive them to leave their homeland or region.

Pull factors

Migrants may be attracted to another country because it has a more stable government or offers more freedom. It may have better work opportunities and a higher standard of living. Migrants might be looking for a better education, or move for family reasons – to be with loved ones.

Push factors

Economic problems are one of the main reasons that people migrate. In Venezuela, the economy collapsed in 2015 and people couldn't meet their basic needs. The country experienced severe political and social crises. In 2020, a shocking 95 per cent – almost the entire population – were living below the poverty line. From 2015 to 2022, more than 7 million Venezuelans abandoned their country, mostly for other Latin American lands. Other major push factors are war and persecution (see pages 10–11).

People protest in Caracas, Venezuela about the shortage of medicines in 2019. The sign says, 'Where are the medicines?'

The River Nile's water levels are rising, causing frequent flooding in Khartoum, Sudan, which destroys homes and kills livestock.

Natural disasters and climate change

Environmental catastrophes force people to move immediately. In China, the Philippines, Bangladesh, India and the USA, people have fled their homes because of devastating floods or typhoons (tropical storms). Other crises develop more slowly. In Sudan, climate change is causing a more extreme climate – severe storms and flooding are more frequent. Farmers' herds of cattle, sheep and goats have grown smaller, farmers no longer have reliable food sources and it has become hard to make a living. Such gradual changes are more likely to increase migration than sudden crises. If farming is becoming too tough, people save up money to migrate.

Competition over scarce natural resources can also help to cause crises. In 2023, civil conflict erupted in Sudan, forcing thousands to flee quickly to neighbouring lands.

CLIMATE-CHANGE MIGRATION

Dozens of villages in Fiji, an island in the South Pacific Ocean, are under severe threat from rising sea levels. The government plans to move the whole population to safer areas. In 2014, the 140 inhabitants of the village of Vunidogoloa were the first to move, packing their belongings on to trucks and heading inland to a hilly area. The move has mostly been a success: the villagers are close to healthcare and schools, have comfortable new homes and can grow food more easily.

WHO ARE MIGRANTS AND WHERE DO THEY GO?

If you're from a stable, high-income country, you can usually move relatively freely. But if you are in a low-income, unstable country, it is difficult to migrate legally to a wealthy land. Around half of international migrants are in low- and middle-income countries.

Border controls

High-income countries tend to have strict rules to control who crosses their borders. Some, such as Canada, Australia and the UK, have a points system. Would-be migrants need to score a certain number of points for their age, level of education and work experience. Skilled people, such as doctors and engineers, can usually get a visa to come. It is trickier for less skilled workers to enter these countries. Border controls are generally not so strict in low- and middle-income countries.

Many migrants and refugees from the Caribbean and Central America, like these Haitians, go to middle-income Mexico, where 40 per cent of the population live in poverty.

Who migrates?

Around 75 per cent of international migrants are of working age – between 15 and 64 years old. About 3 per cent more men migrate than women. Migrants tend to be neither the poorest nor the richest in their country, but they can afford to travel.

Worldwide movement

Migrants are spread all over the world. In Sub-Saharan Africa, Europe and Central Asian countries, most people migrate within the region. This is the case in Latin America, the Caribbean, East Asia and the Pacific too. But many people from all those regions also migrate to North America. Most countries take in migrants while their own citizens move elsewhere too.

A migrant gardening in a Johannesburg home. Many migrants from neighbouring southern African countries move to South Africa, where average incomes are higher.

IT'S A FACT

The top destination countries for migrants in 2020 were the USA, Germany, Saudi Arabia, the Russian Federation and the UK.

MIGRATION CORRIDORS

These 'corridors' are unofficial links between an origin country and a destination country. The biggest in the world is from Mexico to its richer northern neighbour, the USA. In 2020, 11 million Mexicans were living in the USA. Mexicans tend to go to areas with Mexican communities or where they have friends or relatives. Migration is not one-way; many Mexicans later return home.

A traditional Mexican dancer at a festival in San Antonio, Texas, USA, where about half the population are Mexican.

FLEEING DANGER: REFUGEES AND IDPS

Refugees are different to migrants because they have to flee their country rather than leaving by choice. According to the 1951 Convention on the Status of Refugees, a refugee is a person who has fled their country because of a 'well-founded fear of being persecuted for reasons of race, religion, nationality, membership in a particular social group or political opinion.' People who are forced to move to another area of their country are known as Internally Displaced People (IDPs).

Conflict

Most refugees fleeing war cross the border to a nearby country. After Russia invaded Ukraine in 2022, around 8 million Ukrainians fled, mostly to neighbouring lands. Nearby countries sometimes try to stop more refugees coming in. In 2018, the Turkish government built a concrete wall along the border with Syria. Desperate to escape from conflict, Syrians then tried to enter Turkey by climbing the wall, tunnelling under it or bribing Turkish officials – offering them money to allow the refugees through the border.

Ukrainian refugees rest after their journey at a refugee shelter in Przemyśl, Poland, near the Ukrainian border, in March 2022.

IDPs

Civil wars force people to escape within their country. Yemen has endured civil war since 2014, between the Sunni Muslim government and Houthi Shi'a Muslim rebels. Environmental disaster has added to the troubles. In 2020, 300,000 Yemenis lost their homes, crops and animals after catastrophic flooding, and were forced to move away.

The girls in this class in Afghanistan will not be able to go to secondary school under Taliban rules – one reason why over 8 million Afghans have fled their country.

Persecution

People who are persecuted because of their religion, gender or sexuality may be forced to flee their home country. The conflict in Afghanistan has forced millions to leave, but women face particular difficulties and danger. The Taliban government dictates that women are not allowed to attend secondary school or university, to have a job or take part in public life. In nearly 70 countries worldwide, same-sex relationships are illegal. LGBT people may escape to avoid being imprisoned or even put to death for having a relationship.

IT'S A FACT

Syria, Afghanistan and South Sudan produced the highest number of refugees from 2005 to 2020. At the end of 2020, Syria, the Democratic Republic of Congo and Colombia had the largest numbers of people displaced by conflict, followed by Yemen.

HOW MOVING IS GOOD FOR MIGRANTS

Migrants who choose to move usually seek a better standard of living, education and housing. It can be challenging at first, getting used to a different country and possibly a new language, so they might not enjoy the benefits straight away. They hope that life will improve over time.

Work less, earn more

People who move to a wealthier country may be able to enjoy a higher income doing their normal job. Skilled professionals can move relatively easily to another land, especially if they speak the same language. Doctors migrate from the UK to Australia, where working conditions are usually less stressful, they work fewer hours and earn more. Nurses migrate from low-income Jamaica to Canada, the USA and the UK for improved pay and career opportunities.

There are many nurses of Caribbean or African origin working in healthcare around the world.

Opportunities for women

Women who have been to university may migrate to countries where women have more rights, are treated more equally and can earn more money than in their own country.

Better for the children

Many migrants move in the hope that they can create a better future for their children. They may be seeking better access to public services, such as healthcare and education, than in their own country. Young migrants often benefit the most because they enjoy good healthcare from an early age.

The younger the children are, the more easily they tend to settle in a new country, too. They go to school, learn the language quickly and adapt to the local culture.

INTERNATIONAL STUDENTS

Around 6 million students worldwide migrate for education. The most popular destinations are the USA, UK and Australia – where universities have a good reputation. The students generally gain confidence through adapting to a different culture and improving their language and other skills. Some stay and work for a few years afterwards. Having a degree from a high-income country impresses employers, which helps students to find a good job when they return home. Former students may promote trade or other relations between their homeland and the country where they studied.

Schoolchildren in east Germany, including migrant children. As adults, the children of migrants may have similar work opportunities to people born in the country.

DIFFICULTIES FOR MIGRANTS

It can be heart-breaking to leave behind your home, relatives and community. Then you have to adapt to a different way of life in a new country. Irregular migrants, who do not have the legal right to enter a country, face particular difficulties.

Building workers in Stamford, Connecticut, USA pouring concrete. Migrants often do this kind of tough manual work.

Coping with change

Migrants leave behind their community and need to adjust to a new society, culture and often language. At first, even daily activities can be challenging, such as using the roads, going shopping or catching the bus. For those who don't speak the language well, it can be a challenge to get to know people and they may feel lonely and isolated.

The '4 Ds'

Finding a job can be complicated in a new country. Recent migrants often have no choice but to take the '4 Ds' – the dirty, dangerous, difficult and demeaning (making people feel small) jobs that locals don't want to do. In the USA, many migrants work from dawn to dusk in low-paid jobs in construction and agriculture, often in dirty or dangerous conditions. In the Gulf States and Saudi Arabia, South Asians and Filipino women commonly work long hours as house servants for minimal pay.

Even if they are well qualified and speak the language, migrants might not be able to work in their profession – for example, as lawyers or doctors – because their qualifications are not accepted in the new country. They may have to do other jobs, such as driving taxis or working in restaurants, which can feel like a waste of their valuable skills.

Irregular migrants

Some people are unable to migrate to another country legally, for example, because they cannot get a visa. Known as irregular migrants, they live 'under the radar', avoiding contact with officials, who might send them back to their country. They often take any work they can for low pay. It can be a struggle to find a decent home and access healthcare.

What Can I Do?

If there is a new child in your class from another city or country, make them feel welcome. Ask them to sit with you and join in your break-time activities. You could do a class project on where they come from. If they speak a different language, try to learn a few words.

Migrant workers, like these strawberry-pickers in Greece, often take jobs in farming, which do not require them to speak the local language fluently.

HOW MIGRATION HELPS HOST COUNTRIES

Most migrants are fit, healthy, of working age – and prepared to work hard. They tend to be young, educated, and are often productive and innovative. Migrants usually pay more in taxes than they receive in benefits, such as sick pay. They enrich the culture, bringing their food, music, literature and sports customs.

Filling the gaps

Migrants can help economic growth, filling gaps in the workforce. Worldwide, there is a shortage of healthcare workers, made worse by the Covid-19 pandemic. Many governments have encouraged nurses to migrate to work in hospitals and care homes. Migrant health workers make up nearly a fifth of all healthcare workers in the USA and over a tenth in the European Union (EU). Healthcare services depend on them.

लसीकरण विभाग
VACCINATION AREA

Health workers wait for their Covid-19 vaccination in Mumbai, India. Many Indian health workers migrate to richer countries.

Dynamic and innovative

Migrants are often risk-takers – they have left the country they know for a fresh start. In business, they may be more willing to take risks than local people, even though it is harder for them to get business loans. Migrants can achieve highly in innovation, running successful companies, and winning arts and science awards. In the USA, Armenian entrepreneur and inventor Noubar Afeyan, originally from Armenia, is co-founder of the Covid-19 vaccine producer, Moderna. He has been involved in 70 start-up companies and holds more than 100 patents for his inventions.

Migrants and refugees share their food culture. This Iranian-run café in the UK serves Iranian saffron tea as well as regular café drinks.

Sharing culture

A major impact of migration is the sharing of cultures. Migrants bring their food traditions with them, and have opened successful restaurants in many host countries. They have travelled with their music, for example, bringing reggae from Jamaica, and bhangra from India – and they contribute to sports at local, national and international level.

What Can I Do?

Find out about a celebrity from another country, such as a musician, dancer, sportsperson or writer. How did they achieve fame? What challenges did they face? Make a poster to display at school.

PROBLEMS FOR HOST COUNTRIES

If huge numbers of migrants or refugees arrive suddenly, this can put pressure on housing, education and healthcare services. Tensions may arise with local people. In some countries, far-right political organisations blame migrants for social and economic problems.

Crisis

In 2022, around 250,000 migrants and refugees entered Panama in Central America. They included 150,000 people from Venezuela, seeking a better life after the collapse of the Venezuelan economy (see page 6). They travelled through the Darién Gap between Colombia and Panama, a difficult and dangerous journey through the rainforest. The large number of arrivals put a huge strain on Panama's resources. International aid agencies had to step in to help Panama to provide health services, food, fresh water and shelter in the communities hosting the newcomers.

Migrants arrive in Darién province, Panama, 2022 after a gruelling journey of five or six days through swamps, in heat and frequent rain.

In the UK, the lack of local workers to labour long hours picking the fruit and vegetable harvests led to £60-million worth of wasted harvests in 2022.

Taking jobs?

Worldwide, the effects of migration on jobs and wages vary widely, although often migration has little impact. Migrants often do the '4 D' jobs (see page 14) that locals are not prepared to do, such as harvesting fruit and vegetables. But people commonly feel that when migrants arrive, it becomes harder for locals to find a job, and that wages go down because the newcomers work for less money. They may resent migrants.

Rising racism

Far-right political parties, which often want to halt migration, can build on tensions between local people and migrants. They argue that jobs, housing and healthcare are scarce because of migrants and that locals should come first. In some countries, far-right parties have been extremely successful in elections: the anti-migrant Sweden Democrats became the second-largest party in parliament in 2022.

FAKE NEWS

Anti-migrant groups post disinformation (deliberately false information) on social media about migration. In the EU, they spread stories saying more migrants are arriving than there really are, that they damage the economy and commit crime. In 2022, the European Commission established a Code of Practice on Disinformation. Major online platforms, advertisers and research organisations committed to providing more fact-checking of information and stopping adverts that contain disinformation.

What Can I Do?

Learn how to find good sources of information:

1 Use well-known news websites: read the 'about' section if you don't know the site.

2 Check the author: are they an expert and do they give sources for the information?

3 Check the story appears on other well-known news sites.

HELPING THEIR HOMELANDS

If people cannot find jobs in their own country, migration is a useful way to reduce unemployment. Many Indian graduates leave to seek work overseas. Living abroad, migrants contribute to their communities back home through remittances – earnings that they send home. Low-income countries receive around four times more support from remittances than from government aid programmes.

A helping hand

Having a family member working abroad can make the difference between extreme poverty and scraping by. Families in poverty use remittances for basics such as food and shelter. They pay for healthcare and the education of family members – these services are not free in many countries. Mobile money apps, such as the M-Pesa app in Kenya, make it quick and easy to transfer money to relatives back home. Thousands of Kenyans on low incomes have used this money to set up small businesses.

The M-Pesa app allows people to transfer money across Africa, even if they do not have a bank account.

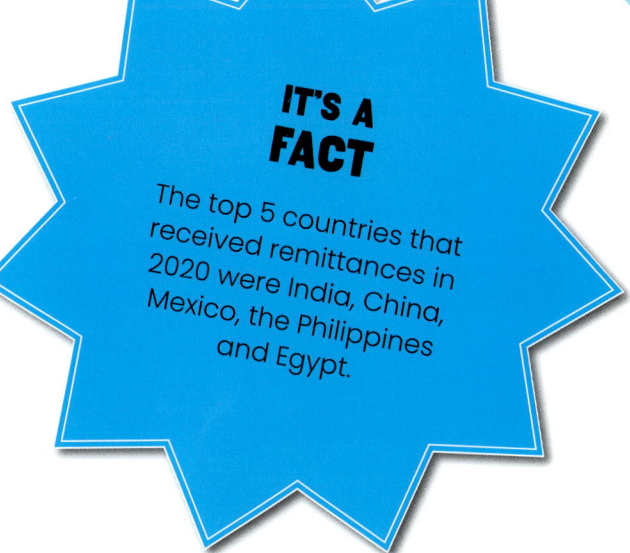

This vegetable stall in Chinatown, New York City, USA sells popular East Asian vegetables, such as Chinese cabbage.

Boosting business

Migrants themselves may set up businesses in their home country, providing jobs and boosting the economy. Their links help to increase trade between their host and home countries. They create a market for imports from their home country. For example, Chinese, Japanese and Thai-owned shops and cafes around the world import foods from East Asia. Migrants may also donate money to create parks and build libraries back home.

Diaspora bonds

During times of financial crisis or after a disaster, governments may raise funds for development projects through diaspora bonds – they borrow money from their citizens who live abroad. The citizens lend money at a lower rate than financial institutions. India and Israel have raised billions of pounds this way.

IT'S A FACT

The top 5 countries that received remittances in 2020 were India, China, Mexico, the Philippines and Egypt.

BRAIN DRAIN AND DEPENDENCE

Although migration brings great benefits, it can have negative effects on home countries if a huge proportion of skilled and educated people leave. This is called the brain drain, and it can make low-income countries even poorer.

Losing talent and taxes

The brain drain leads to a decline in the working-age population and reduces income from taxes. A country may have spent large amounts of money on educating its doctors, nurses and teachers. Then, these highly skilled people leave for a better life elsewhere. They now pay taxes abroad, so the home country does not receive the benefits. Without them, home countries may not be able to run services properly. During a health crisis, such as the Covid-19 pandemic, their already poor healthcare system is stretched to breaking point. Such countries can end up in a vicious circle: as more workers migrate, the economy declines further, which leads to further waves of people migrating.

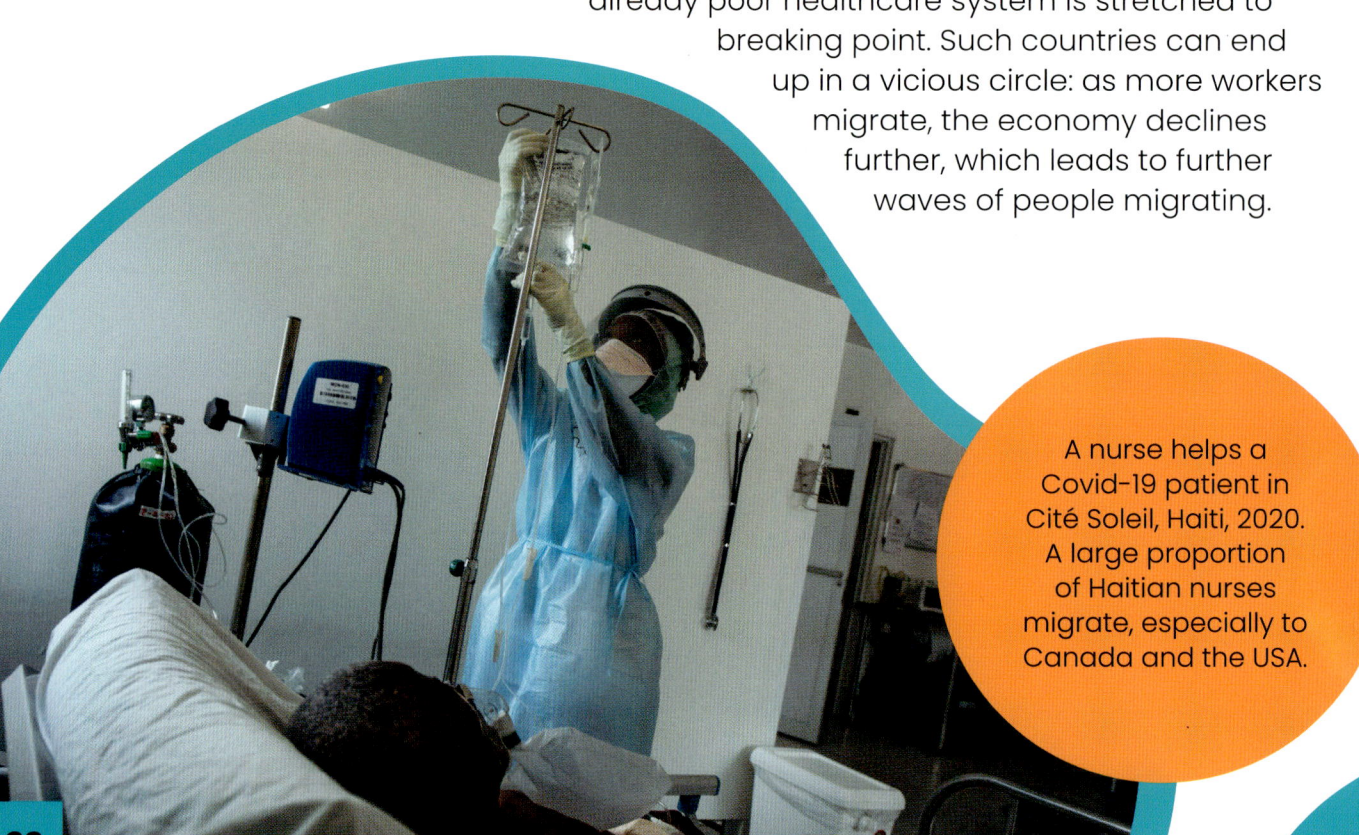

A nurse helps a Covid-19 patient in Cité Soleil, Haiti, 2020. A large proportion of Haitian nurses migrate, especially to Canada and the USA.

Increasing the rich–poor divide

The countries that experience the worst brain drain are small, low-income countries in the tropics, such as Haiti and Jamaica, and those with fewer than 1 million workers. Samoa, in the central South Pacific Ocean, has a population of just 219,000 and the world's highest levels of skilled people leaving the country, as of 2022. A small island economy, Samoa has little manufacturing industry and relies on tourism. People with a degree tend to migrate, while both skilled and unskilled workers move to Australia and New Zealand through Labour Mobility Schemes. The migration of workers from small, low-income nations increases the already wide economic gap between high-income and low-income countries. The host country receives even more highly skilled workers, while the home country loses them.

Attracted by the sunny weather and beautiful beaches, tourists come to Samoa to stay in these traditional beach huts.

REVERSE BRAIN DRAIN

More than 30 million Indians live abroad. Yet since 2020, many have returned – a 'reverse brain drain.' Returning migrants find jobs in India's booming life sciences and healthcare industries, or opportunities with multinational technology and international research organisations. They use their knowledge and experience gained abroad to build family businesses or set up new ones.

BUILDING PEACE

Refugees from war may push for peace while they are abroad and often want to go home as soon as the conflict is over. Once the war has ended, community stabilisation can help to build peace so that people feel safe to return.

Campaigns to end conflict

War refugees often raise awareness of the conflict in their country and campaign for a peaceful solution. Since the outbreak of protests in Iran in 2022 for the rights of women and minority ethnic groups, Iranians (and non-Iranians) worldwide have demonstrated for 'women, life, freedom' in solidarity. They support the struggle against the Iranian government for democracy and equal rights for all.

Protests for women's rights erupted in Iran in 2022 after 22-year-old Mahsa Amini died following her arrest for not wearing a hijab properly.

Syrian refugees live alongside poor Lebanese people in Bab al-Tabbaneh and Jabal Mohsen, Tripoli, some of the poorest areas of Lebanon.

Community stabilisation

Community stabilisation is a way to build peace so that refugees can go home and people do not feel the need to flee. Projects have been set up in countries such as Chad, Somalia, Iraq and Lebanon. They are run in communities affected by crisis to make them stable and secure again. People in an area, sometimes from different sides of a conflict, play a key part in designing and running the projects, which include improving basic services: clean water, healthcare and education.

COMMUNITY STABILISATION IN LEBANON

With a population of about 6 million, Lebanon hosts around 1.5 million Syrian refugees. Tensions have arisen between the Lebanese and the refugees. In poor communities, there were not enough basic services for everyone, and locals blamed the refugees for damage to the environment and crime. In Baal al Darawish, Tripoli, one of the poorest areas of Lebanon, two committees of Syrians and Lebanese, male and female, were trained in conflict resolution, project design and problem-solving. They came up with two actions. The male committee built a basketball court for Lebanese and Syrian youth, creating a safe space for sports and socialising. The women set up a carpentry workshop for women to create handicrafts for sale, giving them an opportunity to make their own living. Through working together, the Lebanese and Syrian communities grew to understand each other better.

CLIMATE-CHANGE ACTION

Taking action on climate change can allow people to survive without migrating. Globally, there are projects to reduce harm to the environment. People can adapt to climate change, for instance, by farming different crops or constructing new buildings in places that are unlikely to be affected by extreme weather events.

A girl takes part in the Green Legacy tree-planting campaign in Ethiopia, in 2020. By 2022, Ethiopians had planted 25 billion tree seedlings.

Tree planting

Planting trees can improve the environment so that people are able to remain on their land. In Ethiopia, the Green Legacy Initiative tree-planting campaign has been running since 2019. Around half of the trees planted in 2022 were for agro-forestry – farmers grew fruit such as avocadoes, and coffee trees on their land. The trees are good for the environment and useful for the farmers, who can sell the fruit. Avocado trees produce increasing amounts of fruit for 25 years and still bear fruit for many years after, so it is worthwhile looking after them.

Adapting to climate change

Sometimes, it is simpler to adapt to climate change than to try to prevent it. In the coastal regions of Bangladesh, cyclones and storm surges are increasing. They flood the land with salty water, making it hard to grow crops. Farmers have adapted to growing salt-tolerant crops – natural plants that can cope with the salt. They include varieties of carrot, potato, cabbage, kohlrabi and beet.

The city of Dar es Salaam, Tanzania, is also prone to flooding. In the rainy season, floods destroy homes. When planning the new ward of Tandale, a city project trained university students and local people to map the areas that were likely to flood so they could improve the drains there and construct buildings elsewhere.

What Can I Do?

Here are some simple actions that can help to reduce climate change.

- Avoid food waste – reheat leftovers the next day.

- Drink tap water instead of bottled drinks.

- Eat less meat.

- Learn to mend your clothes and swap those you don't need any more.

- Turn off devices you are not using.

- Try to only buy things you really need or want.

Farm workers gather salt-tolerant kohlrabi to sell in the local market in Dhaka, Bangladesh.

27

THE FREEDOM OF MOVEMENT DEBATE

Some people argue that since companies are free to set up in other countries, workers should be allowed to work where they like. Others say that countries should control who enters their country. What do you think?

For freedom of movement

Migrants can contribute to the economy, society and culture of their host country. If people have freedom of movement, they can move legally, and do not need to arrange dangerous journeys in secret. They can move from places that lack jobs to places with plenty. If people migrate freely, they can settle quickly, learn the language, start work and pay taxes.

A Lebanese mezze plate with a range of tasty dishes. Lebanese migrants have shared their food culture around the world, including in Europe, America and Australia.

Against freedom of movement

Countries should manage migration. They need tough border controls to prevent being overwhelmed by newcomers. Otherwise, there may not be enough jobs, housing, healthcare or schools for all. Meanwhile, low-income countries with severe brain drain are short of workers for vital jobs in education and healthcare. It is better to focus on developing those countries so that people do not have to migrate for a decent life.

What Can I Do?

At school, hold a debate for and against freedom of movement to help others understand the issues. Hold a vote at the end to find out what most people think.

Heads of state and government at an ECOWAS meeting in Accra, Ghana. ECOWAS aims to allow the free movement of people in the region.

THE EU AND ECOWAS

Some regions of the world already enjoy freedom of movement for people who live in them. The European Union has the Schengen agreement (1985). No border controls exist between member countries. People living in the countries that have signed the agreement can live and work anywhere in the Schengen area. The 15 members of the Economic Community of West African States (ECOWAS) have similar rules, although some countries do not follow them. They may restrict the types of jobs migrants can do; for example, Nigerian street sellers cannot trade in Ghana. ECOWAS needs to work to ensure the rules are followed.

Safe routes

Migration is likely to continue, as it has throughout human history. Whatever policies a country adopts, it seems wise to provide safe, legal routes for migrants to reach other lands, and to protect refugees fleeing danger.

GLOSSARY

agroforestry Farming that includes growing trees

citizen A person with the right to belong to a particular country.

civil war A war between groups of people within the same country.

climate change Long term shifts in the Earth's weather, including changes in temperature, wind patterns and rainfall, especially the increase in the temperature of the Earth's atmosphere.

colonise To take over control of another country, usually by force, and send people from your country to live there.

cyclone A violent tropical storm in which strong winds move in a circle.

democracy A political system in which all adults can vote in elections for the rulers of the country.

far-right political parties Parties whose members tend to believe their country is better than others and often have racist views towards migrants and people from different backgrounds to them.

hijab A head covering that Muslim women may wear outside the home – in a few countries, they have to wear it by law.

homeland The country where a person was born.

host country The country that migrants move to.

Houthi Shia A movement following a different form of Islam from the Sunni majority in Yemen.

imports Goods that are bought from other countries.

innovative Introducing or using new ideas or ways of doing something.

irregular migrant Someone who has moved to a different country outside the laws or rules for entering that country.

patent A document that proves a person has the right to be the only one to make, use or sell a product or an invention.

persecution Treating people badly because of their ethnic group, culture, religious or political beliefs.

qualification An exam that you have passed or a course of study that you have successfully completed.

refugee A person who has been forced to leave their country to escape war, persecution or natural disaster.

stable Steady, and not likely to change or fail.

storm surge An unusual rise in sea level near the coast, caused by wind from a severe storm.

Sunni The larger of the two main branches of Islam. Two-thirds of the people of Yemen are Sunni Muslims.

visa A mark in your passport that gives you permission to enter a country.

FURTHER INFORMATION

Books

The Power of Welcome: Real-life Refugee and Migrant Journeys – a graphic novel by Ada Jusic, Marie Bamyani, Ramzee, Sonya Zhurenko and Nadine Kaadan, Scholastic, 2023

Who are Refugees and Migrants? What Makes People Leave their Homes? And Other Big Questions by Michael Rosen and Annemarie Young, Wayland, 2019

A World Full of Journeys and Migrations: Over 50 stories of human migration that changed our world by Martin Howard and Christopher Corr, Frances Lincoln Children's Books, 2022

Websites

kids.nationalgeographic.com/magazine/article/fake-news
Learn to use good sources of information and how to spot fake news.

www.bbc.co.uk/bitesize/topics/zs2b3j6/articles/z2hptrd
Why people migrate and the impacts of migration

www.unhcr.org/uk/teaching-about-refugees.html
Watch animations about refugees, migrants and internally displaced people.

www.un.org/en/global-issues/migration
United Nations video about history of migration and migration today, and how countries can work together to manage migration well.

INDEX

WHAT CAN WE DO?

TITLES IN THE SERIES

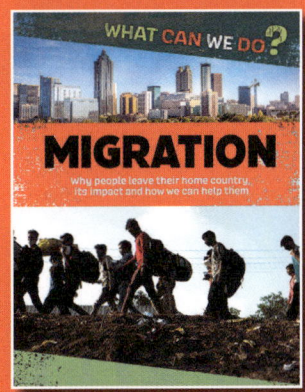